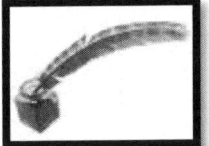

In an age when men dominated the literary world and journalism was almost exclusively a male occupation, Dorothy Parker was an accomplished poet, short story writer, screen writer, fiction and nonfiction author, critic and satirist and a leading American wit. She won two Academy Award nominations, was a founding member of the Algonquin Round Table, was Blacklisted for her political views, went through three marriages (True to her style, two of them were to the same man)

She was known as a person who didn't suffer fools easily and overall she was said to be a difficult person who tried those befriended her with near constant talk of suicide, black depressions spiked by swings of elation. She insulted publishers and editors who gave her deadlines. She could and often did, speak ill of those who spoke well of her. She was more than probably bi-polar which went untreated.

Dorothy set the gauge, the style and attitude or the tough, intelligent urban woman of her day and her poetry was pointed and her short stories were bittersweet, her literary commentary brilliant.

Her life was plagued by challenges...... addictions, creative dry spells, depression, financial woes, a series of betrayals, humiliating adulteries and abandonment by the men she chose to love......and each one seemed, at least on the surface, to defeat her.

Called Dot or Dottie as a child, she was born the fourth child of Dorothy Rothschild to Jacob Henry, a successful garment manufacturer and Eliza Annie Rothschild (née Marston) at 732 Ocean Avenue in the West End village of Long

Branch, New Jersey, where her parents had a summer beach cottage. She was quick to note in her essay "My Hometown" that her parents got her back to their Manhattan apartment shortly after Labor Day so she could be called a true New Yorker.

Long Branch New Jersey 1890

Hers was an unhappy, loveless childhood and Dorothy described herself as "a plain disagreeable child with stringy hair and a yen to write poetry." Dorothy's mother was of Scottish descent, and her father was of German-Jewish descent. But she had ambivalent feelings about her Jewish heritage and joked that she married to escape her name.

Once, when I was young and true,
Someone left me sad-
Broke my brittle heart in two;
And that is very bad.

She grew up on the Upper West Side and attended Roman Catholic elementary school at the Convent of the Blessed Sacrament, despite having a Jewish father and Protestant stepmother. Dorothy was asked to leave the Convent of the Blessed Sacrament following her characterization of the Immaculate Conception as "spontaneous combustion".

"But as for helping me in the outside world, the convent taught me only that if you spit on a pencil eraser it will erase in," she said later.

She attended Miss Dana's School, a finishing school in Morristown, New Jersey. But, for all given purposes, her formal education ended when she was 13.
Her mother died in West End in July 1898, when Parker was a month shy of turning five. Her father remarried in 1900 to a woman named Eleanor Francis Lewis. (She would die five years later in 1903)

Dorothy detested her father and stepmother, accusing her father of being physically abusive and refusing to call Eleanor either "mother" or "stepmother," instead referring to her as "the housekeeper."

"Men seldom make passes at girls who wear glasses". **Dorothy, who, born hopelessly nearsighted, wore glasses since early childhood.**

Following her father's death in 1913, (Her brother Henry died aboard the Titanic a year before her father died) Dorothy played piano at a dancing school to earn a living while she worked on her verse, selling her first poem to *Vanity Fair*

magazine in 1914. Several months later, she was hired as an editorial assistant for another Condé Nast magazine, *Vogue*. She moved to Vanity Fair as a staff writer following two years at *Vogue*. But the *New Yorker Magazine* would be her home for the next 32 years.

PG Woodhouse

In 1916, Dorothy sold several of her poems to Vogue, and was given an editorial position on the magazine. A year later, Dorothy Rothschild became Dorothy Parker in 1917 she met and married a Wall Street stock broker, Edwin Pond Parker II, who was from old Hartford, Connecticut family. They were separated by his army service in World War I. Edwin returned home wounded, an alcoholic, and a morphine addict.

Her career took off while she was writing theatre criticism for Vanity Fair, which she began to do in 1918 as a stand-in for the vacationing P. G. Wodehouse.

Robert Sherwood

It was here that she met Robert Benchley and Robert E. Sherwood, a fellow Harvard Lampoon alumnus of Benchley's. Sherwood, Parker, and Benchley became close, often having long lunches at the Algonquin Hotel. When the editorial managers went on a European trip, the three took advantage of the situation, writing articles mocking the local theatre establishment and offering parodic commentary on a variety of topics, such as the effect of Canadian hockey on United States fashion.

At one point, the Vanity Fair management sent out a memo forbidding the discussion of salaries in an attempt to rein in the staff. Benchley, Parker, and Sherwood responded with a memo of their own, followed by placards around their necks detailing their exact salaries for all to see.

Management attempted to issue "tardy slips" for staff who were late; on one of these, Benchley filled out, in very small handwriting, an elaborate excuse involving a herd of elephants on 44th Street. Eventually, Dorothy was terminated, allegedly due to complaints by the producers of the plays she skewered in her theatrical reviews. Upon learning of her termination, Benchley tendered his own resignation. Word of it was published in Time by Alexander Woollcott, who was at a lunch with Benchley, Parker, and others. Given that Benchley had two children at the time of his resignation, Parker referred to it as "the greatest act of friendship I'd ever seen." By then, the trio, Dorothy, Benchley and Sherwood began lunching at the Algonquin Hotel on a near-daily basis and became founding members of the Algonquin Round Table.

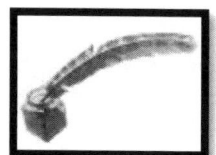

The Algonquin Round Table

'The Round Table thing was greatly overrated. It was full of people looking for a free lunch and asking, "Did you hear the funny thing I said yesterday".' **Dorothy**

"These were no giants. Think who was writing in those days—Lardner, Fitzgerald, Faulkner and Hemingway. Those were the real giants. The Round Table was just a lot of people telling jokes and telling each other how good they were. Just a bunch of loudmouths showing off, saving their gags for days, waiting for a chance to spring them....There was no truth in anything they said. It was the terrible day of the wisecrack, so there didn't have to be any truth..." **Dorothy on the Algonquin Round Table**

"Silly of me to blame it on dates, but so it happened to be. Dammit, it was the Twenties, and we had to be smarty." — **Dorothy**

Founding members of the Algonquin Round Table :(l-r) Art Samuels, Charlie MacArthur, Harpo Marx, Dorothy Parker, and Alexander Woollcott

The Algonquin Round Table was a celebrated group of New York City writers, critics, actors and wits. Gathering initially as part of a practical joke, members of "The Vicious Circle", as they dubbed themselves, met for lunch each day at the Algonquin Hotel from 1919 until roughly 1929. At these luncheons they engaged in wisecracks, wordplay and witticisms that, through the newspaper columns of Round Table members, were disseminated across the country.

In its ten years of association, the Round Table and a number of its members acquired national reputations both for their contributions to literature and for their sparkling wit. The group that would become the Round Table began meeting in June 1919 as the result of a practical joke carried out by theatrical press agent John Peter Toohey. Toohey, annoyed at New York Times drama critic Alexander Woollcott for refusing to plug one of Toohey's clients in his column, organized a luncheon supposedly to welcome Woollcott back from World War I, where he had been a correspondent for Stars and Stripes. Instead Toohey used the occasion to poke fun at Woollcott on a number of fronts. Woollcott's enjoyment of the joke and the success of the event prompted Toohey to suggest that the group in attendance meet at the Algonquin each day for lunch.

The group first gathered in the Algonquin's Pergola Room (now called The Oak Room) at a long rectangular table. As they increased in number, Algonquin manager Frank Case moved them to the Rose Room and a round table.

Initially the group called itself "The Board" and the luncheons "Board meetings." After being assigned a waiter named Luigi, the group re-christened itself "Luigi Board." Finally they became "The Vicious Circle" although "The Round Table" gained wide currency after cartoonist Edmund Duffy of the Brooklyn Eagle caricatured the group sitting at a round table and wearing armor.

In addition to the daily luncheons, members of the Round Table worked and associated with each other almost constantly. The group was devoted to games, including cribbage and poker. The group had its own poker club, the Thanatopsis Literary and Inside Straight Club, which met at the hotel on Saturday nights. Regulars at the game included Kaufman, Adams, Broun, Ross and Woollcott, with non-Round Tablers Herbert Bayard Swope, silk merchant Paul Hyde Bonner, baking heir Raoul Fleischmann, actor Harpo Marx, and writer Ring Lardner sometimes sitting in.

Members often visited Neshobe Island, a private island co-owned by several "Algonks"— but governed by Aleck Woollcott as a "benevolent tyrant," as his biographer Samuel Hopkins Adams charitably put it— located on several acres in the middle of Lake Bomoseen in Vermont. There they would engage in their usual array of games including Wink murder, which they called simply "Murder", plus croquet.

Given the literary and theatrical activities of the Round Table members, it was perhaps inevitable that they would write and stage their own revue, called No Sirree!, staged for one night only in April 1922, was a take-off of a then-popular European touring revue called La Chauve-Souris, directed by Nikita Balieff.

With the success of No Sirree! the Round Tablers hoped to duplicate it with an "official" Vicious Circle production open to the public with material performed by professional actors. Kaufman and Connelly funded the revue, named The Forty-niners. The revue opened in November 1922 and was a failure, running for just 15 performances.

Not all of their contemporaries were fans of the group. Their critics accused them of logrolling, or exchanging favorable plugs of one another's works, and of rehearsing their witticisms in advance.

James Thurber was a detractor of the group, accusing them of being too consumed by their elaborate practical jokes. H. L. Mencken, who was much admired by many in the Circle, was also a critic, commenting to fellow writer Anita Loos that "their ideals were those of a vaudeville actor, one who is extremely 'in the know' and inordinately trashy."

Groucho Marx, brother of Round Table associate Harpo, was never comfortable amidst the viciousness of the Vicious Circle. "The price of admission is a serpent's tongue and a half-concealed stiletto."

Round Table members and associates did contribute significantly and enduringly to the literary landscape, including Pulitzer Prize-winning work by Circle members Kaufman, Connelly and Sherwood (who won four) and by associate Ferber, and the continuing legacy of Ross's New Yorker. Others made lasting contributions to the realms of stage and screen, not least of which are the films of Harpo and the Marx Brothers and Benchley, and Parker herself has remained renowned for her short stories and literary reviews.

As members of the Round Table moved into ventures outside New York City, inevitably the group drifted apart. By the early 1930s the Vicious Circle was broken. Edna Ferber said she realized it when she arrived at the Rose Room for lunch one day in 1932 and found the group's table occupied by a family from Kansas. Frank Case was asked what happened to the group. He shrugged and replied, "What became of the reservoir at Fifth Avenue and Forty-Second Street? These things do not last forever."

Members of the Round Table

Franklin P. Adams (1881–1960): Columnist at the New York Tribune, the New York World, and the New York Evening Post; wrote the "Always in Good Humor" and "The Conning Tower" columns. Always known as FPA.

Robert Benchley (1889–1945): Vanity Fair managing editor, Life drama editor, humorist and actor in short films.

Heywood Broun (1888–1939): Sportswriter at New York Tribune, columnist at New York World, author; helped found Newspaper Guild.

Marc Connelly (1890–1980): Newspaperman turned playwright; co-wrote plays with George S. Kaufman. Won Pulitzer Prize for play The Green Pastures.

Edna Ferber (1887–1968): Novelist and playwright. Co-wrote plays with George S. Kaufman, including Dinner at Eight. Won Pulitzer Prize for her novel So Big. Wrote Show Boat, Saratoga Trunk, Cimarron, and Giant.

Margalo Gillmore (1897–1986): Actress and "the baby of the Round Table." Starred in early Eugene O'Neill plays.

Jane Grant (1892–1972): First female New York Times general assignment reporter; cofounded The New Yorker with husband Harold Ross.

Ruth Hale (1887–1934): Broadway press agent, helped pass Nineteenth Amendment for women's rights, married Heywood Broun. Fought to use her maiden name professionally.

Beatrice B. Kaufman (1894–1945): Editor, writer, socialite. Married to George.

George S. Kaufman (1889–1961): Playwright, New York Times drama editor, producer, director, actor. Wrote forty-five plays (twenty-six hits), won two Pulitzer Prizes.

Margaret Leech Pulitzer (1894–1974): Magazine short story writer turned serious historian. Married Ralph Pulitzer; after his death, she earned two Pulitzer Prizes in history.

Neysa McMein (1888–1949): Popular magazine cover illustrator, painter.

Herman J. Mankiewicz (1897–1953): Press agent, early New Yorker drama critic; co-wrote plays with Kaufman, produced Marx Brothers movies. Won an Oscar for co-writing Citizen Kane.

Harpo Marx (1888–1964): Actor, comedian, musician, card player.

William B. Murray (1890–1949): Writer and publicist. Murray was a music critic on the Brooklyn Eagle and later head of radio sponsorships at William Morris.

Brock Pemberton (1885–1950): Broadway producer and director. Wrote short stories.

Murdock Pemberton (1888–1982): Broadway press agent, first art critic for The New Yorker.

Harold Ross (1892–1951): Founded The New Yorker with his wife, Jane Grant. He ran the magazine from 1925 until his death.

Arthur H. Samuels (1888–1938): Editor of Harper's Bazaar.

Robert E. Sherwood (1896–1955): Vanity Fair drama editor, Life editor, author, playwright who won four Pulitzer Prizes. Won Oscar for writing The Best Years of Our Lives.

Laurence Stallings (1895–1968): Ex-reporter, editorial writer for New York World. Collaborated with Maxwell Anderson on What Price Glory?

Donald Ogden Stewart (1894–1980): Author, playwright, screenwriter. Red Scare led to him being blacklisted and barred from United States. Won Oscar for The Philadelphia Story.

Frank Sullivan (1892–1976): Journalist turned humorist. A member of *The World*, he was a longtime contributor to The New Yorker.

Deems Taylor (1886–1966): Music critic turned populist composer. Wrote libretto for The King's Henchmen with Edna St. Vincent Millay. Started national concert series. Narrator of Disney classic Fantasia.

John Peter Toohey (1880–1946): Theater press agent for Dinner at Eight, You Can't Take It with You, Of Mice and Men, The Man Who Came to Dinner.

David Wallace (1889–1955): Theatrical press agent.

John V. A. Weaver (1893–1938): Poet who wrote in street vernacular, literary editor of the Brooklyn Eagle; married Peggy Wood.

Peggy Wood (1892–1978): Actress in musical comedies, plays, early TV star.

Alexander Woollcott (1887–1943): Drama critic for New York Times and New York World, CBS radio star as the Town Crier, model for the character of Sheridan Whiteside in Kaufman and Hart's "The Man Who Came to Dinner".

The Round Table at the Algonquin

"It serves me right for keeping all my eggs in one bastard." **This remark was supposedly made by Dorothy after her affair with with playwright, Charles MacArthur which resulted in a pregnancy which she aborted. Dorothy had numerous affairs, before, during and after her marriages. MacArthur was friends with members of the Algonquin Round Table and shared an apartment with Dorothy's other lover Robert Benchley.**

MacArthur's second marriage was to the stage and screen actress, Helen Hayes, from 1928 until his death.

Their adopted son, James MacArthur, was also an actor, best known for playing "Danny Williams" on the American television series Hawaii Five-O.
His brother, John D. MacArthur, was an insurance-company owner and executive, and founded the John D. and Catherine T. MacArthur Foundation, the

benefactor of the "genius awards". Following her affair with MacArthur a depression culminated in her first attempt at suicide. She and Edwin divorced in 1928.

Affairs with both Benchley (Left) and Woollcott (Right) are alleged to have resulted in pregnancies as well as did her affair with the publisher Seward Collins, a self-described "Fascist" and fan of Adolf Hitler who defended the Nazi's oppression of the Jews by saying "It is not persecution. The Jews make trouble. It is necessary to segregate them."

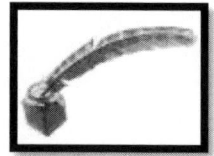

The Great Years

Harold Ross

When Harold Ross founded The New Yorker in 1925, Dorothy and Benchley were part of a "board of editors" established by Ross to allay concerns of his investors. Dorothy's first piece for the magazine appeared in its second issue.

   The next 15 years would be her most productive and successful. In the 1920s alone she published some 300 poems and free verses in outlets including the aforementioned Vanity Fair, Vogue, "The Conning Tower" and The New Yorker along with Life, McCall's and The New Republic.

   She also published her first volume of poetry, Enough Rope, a collection of previously published work along with new material in 1926. The collection sold a remarkable 47,000 copies and garnered impressive reviews. The Nation described her verse as "caked with a salty humor, rough with splinters of disillusion, and tarred with a bright black authenticity."

Although some critics, notably the New York Times, dismissed her work as "flapper   verse," the volume helped cement her status, as the New York World review put it, as "one of the most sparkling wits who express themselves through light verse."

 Dorothy released two more volumes of verse, Sunset Gun (1928) and Death and Taxes (1931), along with the short story collections Laments for the Living (1930) and After Such Pleasures (1933). Not So Deep as a Well (1936) collected much of the material previously published in Rope, Gun and Death and she re-released the fiction with a few new pieces in 1939 under the title Here Lies.

In 1924, she collaborated with fellow Algonquinite George S. Kaufman on a one-act play, Business is Business and later collaborated with playwright Elmer Rice to create Close Harmony. The play was well received in out-of-town previews and was favorably reviewed in New York but closed after a run of just 24 performances. It did, however, become a successful touring production under the title The Lady Next Door.

Elmer Rice

Her best-known short story, "Big Blonde", published in The Bookman magazine, was awarded the O. Henry Award as the best short story of 1929. Her short stories, though often witty, were also spare and incisive, and more bittersweet than comic.

It was also during this time that Dorothy adopted the moniker "Constant Reader" when she wrote book reviews for The New Yorker in the late 1920s and early 1930s, and was known for her humor, wit, and vicious critiques of second- and third-rate novels.

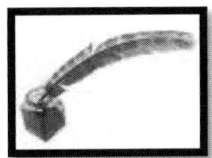

Dorothy in Hollywood

In 1929, the Algonquin Round Table quit meeting for lunch and Dorothy's personal and professional life changed almost completely. Four year later she met a bit actor named Alan Campbell, who was 11 years her junior. They married and moved to Los Angeles during Hollywood's Golden Age.

She and Campbell became a screenplay writing team for the big studios, churning out forgettable scripts for films that went nowhere but all for incredible money. In fact, Hollywood, enamored by Parker's reputation as a leading New York-writer-intellectual-wit, paid her so much money that she verse and poetry writing came to a virtual end. However, Dorothy was a productive out west as she was in New York. In 1936, she contributed lyrics for the song "I Wished on the Moon", with music by Ralph Rainger. (Below)

The song was introduced in The Big Broadcast of 1936 by Bing Crosby. With Robert Carson and Campbell, she wrote the script for the 1937 film *A Star is Born*, which brought them a nomination for Academy Award for Best Writing in Screenplay. She also wrote additional dialogue for *The Little Foxes* in 1941 and received another Oscar nomination, with Frank Cavett, for *Smash-Up*.

Frank Cavett

Dorothy lived in LA, off and on, from 1934 to the 1950s, sharing her time between her New York apartment and her country home in magnificent Bucks County, Pennsylvania. She returned to Manhattan permanently after Alan Campbell's death in June 1963 in their West Hollywood home.

Dorothy Parker and her husband Alan Campbell, at their farmhouse in Bucks County, Pennsylvania, bought largely with the proceeds from their screenwriting in Hollywood where she earned up to $5,000 a week. She married Campbell in 1934 even though he was her junior by 11 years and was widely known, even by Dorothy, as an active bisexual. ("He's as queer as a goddamn Billy goat" she once shouted about Campbell) The couple moved to Hollywood and signed dozens of short-term contracts with Paramount Pictures, and worked as freelancers for various other studios.

Her marriage to Campbell, who, like Dorothy was Jewish and Scots, was tempestuous, with tensions exacerbated by Parker's increasing alcohol intake and spells of verbal abuse and Alan's long-term affair with a married woman while he was in Europe during World War II.

They divorced in 1947, and then remarried in 1950, and remained married (although they lived apart from 1952–1961) When Dorothy returned to Hollywood and reconciled again with Campbell. They worked together on a number of unproduced projects; among her last was an unproduced film for Marilyn Monroe. Parker found Campbell dead in their home in West Hollywood 1963, a suicide by drug overdose.

At Webster Hall in Manhattan in 1938 with husband Allan Campbell

Sid and Laura Perelman helped Dorothy and Campbell buy the run-down farm in Bucks County, where many of New York's literati had chosen to settle. "We haven't any roots, Alan" Parker had complained to Campbell. Dorothy had met S.J. Perelman at a party in 1932, and despite a rocky start (Perelman called it 'a scarifying ordeal')—they remained friends for the next 35 years and lived near each other in Bucks County.

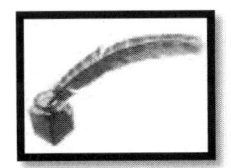

Dorothy on Hollywood

"The only ism Hollywood believes in is plagiarism." **Dorothy**

"I'd like to have money. And I'd like to be a good writer. These two can come together, and I hope they will, but if that's too adorable, I'd rather have money," **Dorothy**

"Hollywood money isn't money. Its congealed snow, melts in your hand, and there you are." **Dorothy**

"I can't talk about Hollywood. It was a horror to me when I was there and it's a horror to look back on. I can't imagine how I did it. When I got away from it I couldn't even refer to the place by name. Out there, I called it." **Dorothy**

"When I dwelt in the East I had my opinion of writing for the screen. I regarded it with a sort of benevolent contempt, as one looks at the raggedy printing of a backward six-year-old. I thought it had just that much relationship to literature. Well, I found out, and I found out hard, and found out forever. Through the sweat and the tears I shed over my first script, I saw a great truth - one of those eternal, universal truths that serve to make you feel much worse than you did when you started. And that is that no writer, whether he writes from love or from money, can condescend to what he writes. What makes it harder in screenwriting is the money he gets. You see, it brings out the uncomfortable little thing called conscience. You aren't writing for the love of it or the art of it or whatever; you are doing a chore assigned to you by your employer and whether or not he might fire you if you did it slackly makes no matter you've got yourself to face, and you have to live with yourself. "**Dorothy**

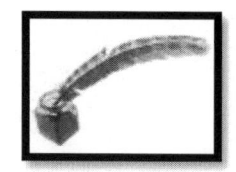

During the 1930s and 1940s, she became an increasingly vocal advocate for civil liberties and civil rights causes and a frequent critic of government. She reported on the Loyalist cause in Spain for the Communist *New Masses* magazine in 1937 and at the request of Soviet Agent Otto Katz and Willi Muenzenberg, a German Communist Party agent, (Katz was actually a Czech and an aide to Muenzenberg) Dorothy helped to found the *Hollywood Anti-Nazi League* in 1936.

Willi Muenzenberg who was later murdered by the Soviet NKVD agents or by party members acting on Stalin's orders.

The League, essentially a front for the Kremlin, grew to 4,000 wealthy and largely clueless members. She also served as chair of the Joint Anti-Fascist Rescue Committee and organized *Project Rescue Ship* to transport Loyalist veterans to Mexico, headed Spanish Children's Relief and lent her name to many other left-wing causes and organizations.

"Now, look, baby, 'Union' is spelled with 5 letters. It is not a four-letter word." **Dorothy to the FBI. Dorothy had a lifelong commitment to causes, most of them with a left bent. She traveled to Boston in 1927 to protest at the Sacco and Vanzetti, the two Italian immigrant anarchists accused, wrongly it turned out, of murdering a guard during a burglary. Dorothy was arrested and charged with "loitering and sauntering", paid a $5.00 fine and returned to New York.**

Listen, I can't even get my dog to stay down. Do I look like someone who could overthrow the government? **Under interrogation by the FBI. Dorothy was listed as a Communist by the publication Red Channels in 1950. The FBI compiled a 1,000-page dossier on her because of her suspected involvement in Communism during the McCarthy era. As a result, she was placed on the Hollywood blacklist by the movie studio bosses. She was eventually called before the House on un-American Activities and pleaded the first instead of the fifth, refusing to name any names. In 1952-1953 testimony was given against her before the HUAC by a variety of people but the committee had long since lost interest in her.**

"When I dwelt in the East I had my opinion of writing for the screen. I regarded it with a sort of benevolent contempt, as one looks at the raggedy printing of a backward six-year-old. I thought it had just that much relationship to literature. Well, I found out, and I found out hard, and found out forever. Through the sweat and the tears I shed over my first script, I saw a great truth - one of those eternal, universal truths that serve to make you feel much worse than you did when you started. And that is that no writer, whether he writes from love or from money, can condescend to what he writes. What makes it harder in screenwriting is the money he gets. You see, it brings out the uncomfortable little thing called conscience. You aren't writing for the love of it or the art of it or whatever; you are doing a chore assigned to you by your employer and whether or not he might fire you if you did it slackly makes no matter. You've got yourself to face, and you have to live with yourself." **Dorothy on why he detested screenwriting**

"She runs the gamut of emotions from A to B." **Dorothy on Katharine Hepburn.**

"The people want democracy - real democracy, Mr. Dies, and they look toward Hollywood to give it to them because they don't get it any more in their newspapers. And that's why you're out here, Mr. Dies - that's why you want to destroy the Hollywood progressive organizations - because you've got to control this medium if you want to bring fascism to this country." **Dorothy to Martin Dies of the House Un-American Activities Committee. In was during her Hollywood years, that Dorothy became political, or at the least showed, her political side. She was a major supporter of the Screenwriters union; enough so that there is a painting of her in its offices today**

Screen and TV Credits

2009 You Were Perfectly Fine

2008 The Sexes

2004 The Game

1999 The Lovely Leave

1996 T'odio, amor meu

1995 The Flower of My Secret

1990 Women and Men: Stories of Seduction

1980 Big Blonde

1975 Ladies of the Corridor

1967 Een heel kleintje maar

1966 Teatterituokio
Nainen, Jumala ja puhelin

1960 ITV Play of the Week
Ladies of the Corridor
Pakinateatteri
Olit aivan mainio

1954 A Star Is Born

1952 Grande Teatro Tupi
A Amiga
A Valsa
De Nova York para Detroit

1951 Queen for a Day

1949 The Fan

1947 Smash-Up: The Story of a Woman

1942 Saboteur

1941 Weekend for Three

The Little Foxes

1938 Trade Winds
Sweethearts

The Cowboy and the Lady

With child actor Dickie Van Patton, later called Dick Van Patton

1937 Woman Chases Man

A Star Is Born

1936 Three Married Men
Lady Be Careful
Suzy
The Moon's Our Home

1935 Hands Across the Table

1934 Here Is My Heart

1920 Remodeling Her Husband

In 1943, Dorothy and Alexander Woollcott collaborated to produce an anthology of her work as part of a series published by Viking Press for servicemen stationed overseas.

Woollcott, who described himself as 'the best writer in America', but with nothing in particular to say". He died while on a CBS Radio program "The People's

Platform" discussing the subject "Is Germany Incurable?" Woollcott commented that he was feeling ill, but continued his remarks. "It's a fallacy to think that Hitler was the cause of the world's present woes," he said. Woollcott continued, adding "Germany was the cause of Hitler." He then suffered a heart attack and died at New York's Roosevelt Hospital a few hours later. He was buried in Clinton, New York, at his alma mater, Hamilton College, but not without some confusion. By mistake, his ashes were sent to Colgate University in Hamilton, New York. When the error was corrected and the ashes were forwarded to Hamilton College, they arrived with 67¢ postage due.

Released in 1944 under the title The Portable Dorothy Parker, the book, which part of the Viking Portable series, had an introduction by Somerset Maugham and included over two dozen of Dorothy's short stories and elected poems from Enough Rope, Sunset Gun, and Death and Taxes. It remains one of only three of the Portable series, the other two being William Shakespeare and The Bible, to remain continuously in print. Woollcott didn't live long enough to see the new edition: he had died in early 1943, at age 56.

In 1952 Dorothy moved back to her beloved New York, into the Volney residential hotel. By then her Round Table friends had scattered and her off again on again relationship with the married Robert Benchley seemed hopelessly strained. She threw herself into a play with co-writer Arnaud d'Usseau, called Ladies of the Corridor that opened in October of 1953 and mercifully closed after six weeks. Shortly afterwards, d'Usseau appeared before the House Un-American Activities Committee, refused to name names and fled to Europe.

Dorothy worked in radio for a while, as a guest panelist on the program *Author, Author* and as a paid writer for radio personalities and novelist Ilka Chase (left below) and Tallulah Bankhead. (right)

She continued writing book reviews as well and from 1957 to 1962 she wrote reviews for Esquire, although these pieces were increasingly erratic because of her worsening addiction to alcohol.

She became more and more secluded towards the end, enough so, that the The Paris Review sent a reporter to find her living in a hotel in midtown with a fluffy white poodle, still throwing out barbs.

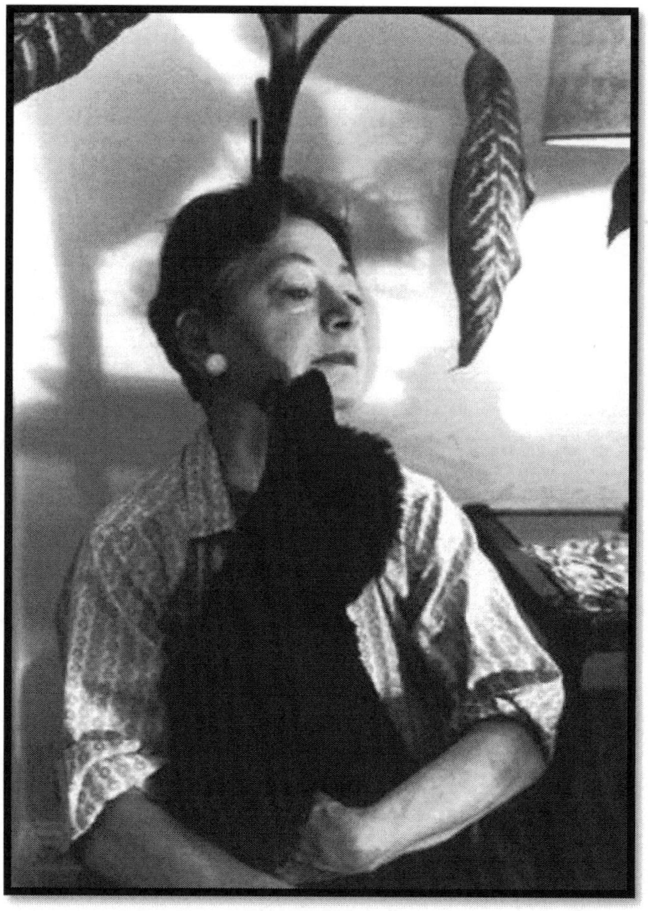

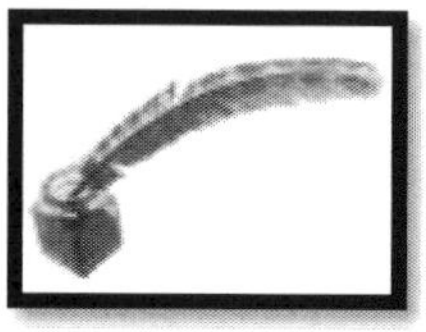

"If I had any decency, I'd be dead. All my friends are." **Dorothy when asked at her 70th birthday party on what she planned to do next.**

Dorothy died in 1967 at age 73 of a heart attack in her apartment at the Volney; a residential hotel located at 23 East 74th Street between Fifth and Madison avenues on New York's fashionable Upper East Side.

Hellman

Lillian Hellman, the writer who Dorothy considered her most trusted confident was named executor of her will and was instructed to leave Dorothy's entire estate to the civil rights leader, Dr. Martin Luther King and, in the event of his death, to the NAACP, including all literary rights. She had no heirs at all. But Hellman, being Hellman, refused to release any of Parker's papers and in large part because of Hellman's medaling, Dorothy's ashes were left unburied for decades, in a file draw in her lawyers office for two decades.

Hellman

Dorothy had not only written her own will, she also designed her own demise. She left orders to be cremated, and she was, on June 9, 1967, at Ferncliff Crematory in Hartsdale, New York. But Hellman, who made all the funeral arrangements, (Dorothy expressly did not want a funeral) never told the crematory what to do with the ashes. So the writer's ashes were stored in Hartsdale until July 16, 1973, when they were mailed to Dorothy's lawyer's offices, O'Dwyer and Bernstein, 99 Wall Street. Paul O'Dwyer, her attorney, took the ashes and stored them in his office where they sat for the next 15 years, in a filing cabinet.
As for Dorothy's paper, they were never found and the speculation is that Hellman, outraged at not having been left any money...the estate was worth about $20,000, a tidy sum at the time.... by Dorothy, destroyed the papers
Hellman went to court to fight the NAACP over the Parker's literary estate but not only did she lose the case, in 1972, the judge also ruled that she should be removed from executorship. In interview after interview, Hellman was adamant that should have gotten the estate and that Dorothy was drunk when she drew up her own will.
Finally, in 1988, the NAACP in claimed Dorothy's ashes and designed a memorial garden for them outside their headquarters in Baltimore, Maryland.
The New York papers ran stories about Dorothy's ashes being stored in round urn in her lawyer's office for 21 years and finally the NAACP stepped in and took the

box from Paul O'Dwyer's law office. The NAACP built a memorial garden at the national headquarters in Baltimore, and interred the ashes there.

On Oct. 20, 1988, the president of the NAACP, Benjamin Hooks, dedicated the memorial garden on the office property. The inscription reads

"Here lie the ashes of Dorothy Parker (1893-1967) Humorist, writer, critic, defender of human and civil rights."

For her epitaph, Dorothy suggested "Excuse My Dust".

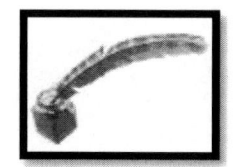

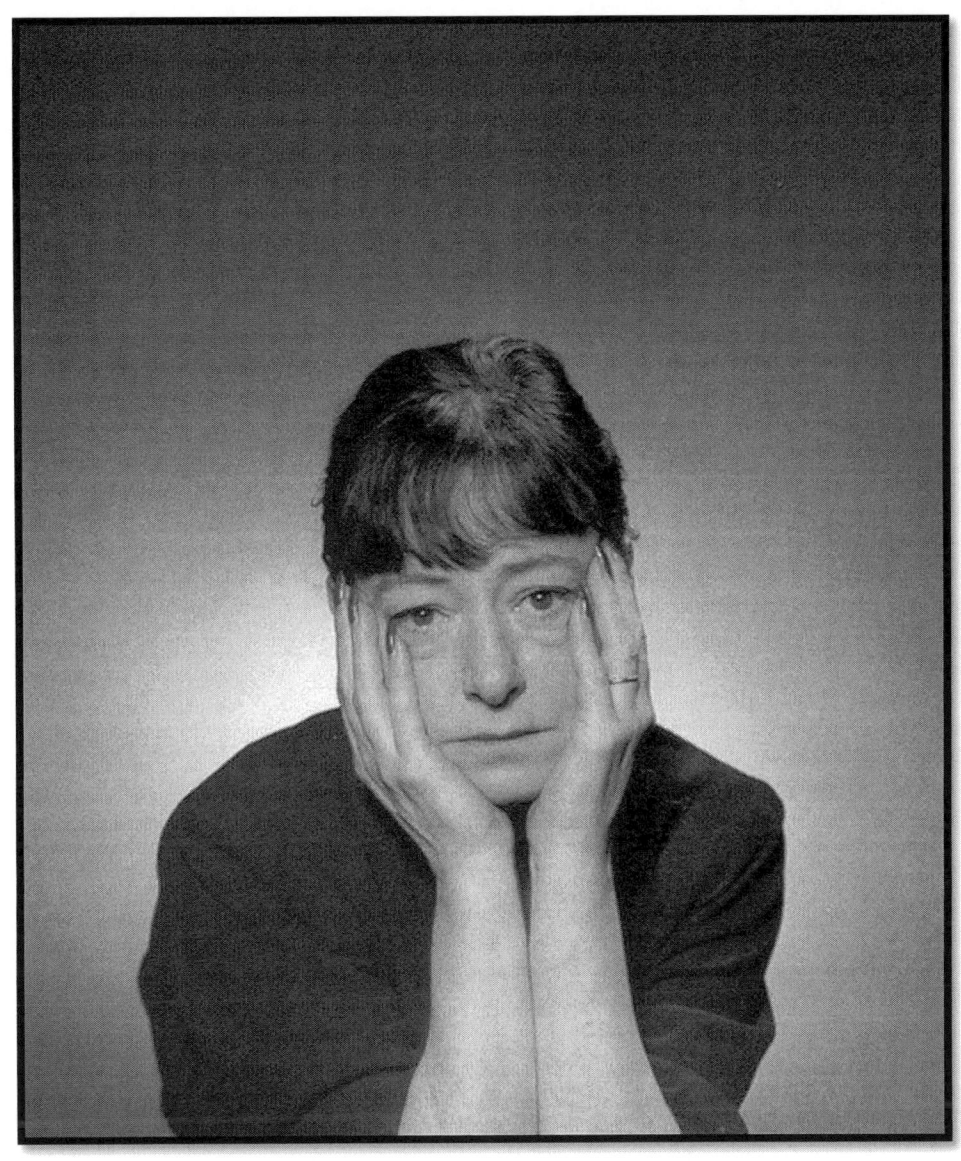

Razors pain you; rivers are damp; acids stain you; and drugs cause cramp. Guns aren't lawful; nooses give; gas smells awful; you might as well live

The Quotable Dorothy

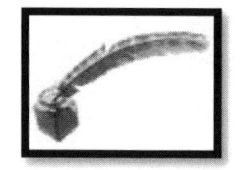

Art is a form of catharsis.

A girl's best friend is her mutter.

A little bad taste is like a nice dash of paprika.

All those writers who write about their childhood! Gentle God, if I wrote about mine you wouldn't sit in the same room with me.

All I need is room enough to lay a hat and a few friends.

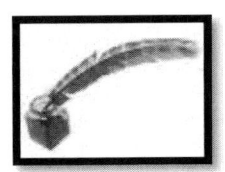

Beauty is only skin deep, but ugly goes clean to the bone

Brevity is the soul of lingerie.

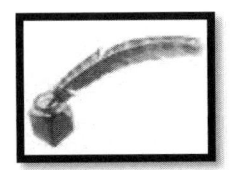

Congratulations, I knew you had it in you. **On a card to a friend who had just given birth**

Clare Boothe Luce, holding a door open for Dorothy: Age before beauty.
Dorothy: Pearls before swine.

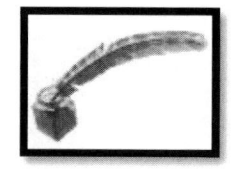

Ducking for apples -- change one letter and it's the story of my life.

Drink and dance and laugh and lie, Love, the reeling midnight through, For tomorrow we shall die! (But, alas, we never do.)

Don't look at me in that tone of voice.

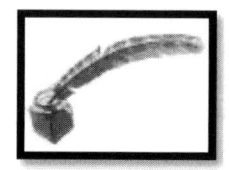

Enjoyed it! One more drink and I'd have been under the host.

Every love's the love before in a duller dress

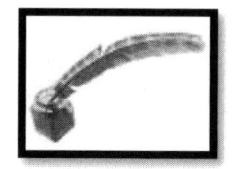

Four be the things I'd have been better without: Love, curiosity, freckles and doubt.

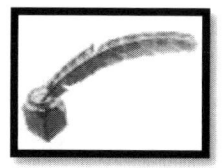

Gratitude -- the meanest and most sniveling attribute in the world.

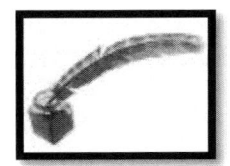

Heterosexuality is not normal, it's just common.

How do people go to sleep? I'm afraid I've lost the knack. I might try busting myself smartly over the temple with the nightlight.

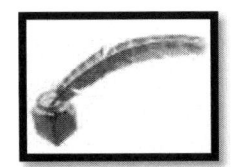

I require three things in a man. He must be handsome, ruthless, and stupid.

I don't care what anybody says about me as long as it isn't true.

I hate writing. But I love having written.

I shall stay the way I am because I do not give a damn.

I'm too fucking busy and vice versa

I'd rather have a bottle in front of me than a frontal lobotomy.

I'm never going to be famous. I don't do anything, not one single thing. I used to bite my nails, but I don't even do that anymore.

I don't care what is written about me so long as it isn't true.

I'd rather have a bottle in front of me than a frontal lobotomy.

I know this will come as a shock to you, Mr. Goldwyn, but in all history, which has held billions and billions of human beings, not a single one ever had a happy ending.

I was always sweet, at first. Oh, it's so easy to be sweet to people before you love them.

If all the young ladies who attended the Yale prom were laid end to end, no one would be the least surprised.

I might repeat to myself slowly and soothingly, a list of quotations beautiful from minds profound - if I can remember any of the damn things.

I require only three things of a man. He must be handsome, ruthless and stupid.

I wish I could drink like a lady I can take one or two at the most three and I'm under the table four and I'm under the host.

I've never been a millionaire but I just know I'd be darling at it.

Idleness, sorrow, a friend, and a foe.

If you want to know what God thinks of money, just look at the people he gave it to.

If you're going to write, don't pretend to write down. It's going to be the best you can do, and it's the fact that it's the best you can do that kills you.

I shall stay the way I am because I do not give a damn.

I find her anecdotes more efficacious than sheep-counting, rain on a tin roof, or alanol tablets.... you will find me and Morpheus, off in a corner, necking.

If all the girls who attend the Vassar were laid end to end, I wouldn't be a bit surprised.

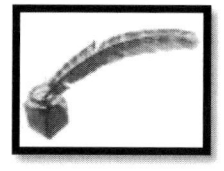

Love is like quicksilver in the hand. Leave the fingers open and it stays. Clutch is, and it darts away.

Lonely is a man without love.

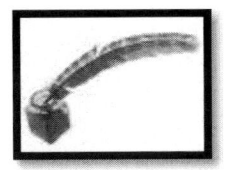

Men don't like nobility in woman. Not any men. I suppose it is because the men like to have the copyrights on nobility -- if there is going to be anything like that in a relationship.

Misfortune and recited misfortune especially, may be prolonged to that point where it ceases to excite pity and arouses only irritation.

Money cannot buy health, but I'd settle for a diamond-studded wheelchair.

Money was made, not to command our will, But all our lawful pleasures to fulfill. Shame and woe to us, if we our wealth obey; The horse doth with the horseman away.

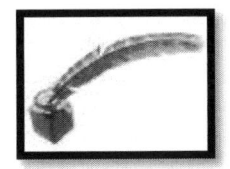

Once in her long-running feud with

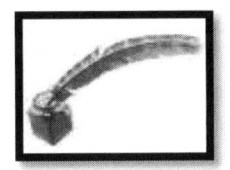

People are more fun than anybody.

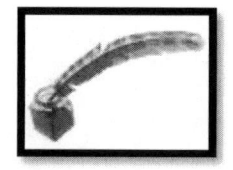

Salary is no object; I want only enough to keep body and soul apart.

Scratch a lover, and find a foe.

Sorrow is tranquility remembered in emotion.

Scratch a lover, and find a foe.

Sometimes I think I'll give up trying, and just go completely Russian and sit on a stove and moan all day.

Some of these you've heard; now you know who said them first

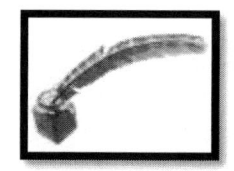

Take care of the luxuries and the necessities will take care of themselves.

Take me or leave me; or, as is the usual order of things, both.

That would be a good thing for them to cut on my tombstone: Wherever she went, including here, it was against her better judgment.

The plot is so tired that even this reviewer, who in infancy was let drop by a nurse with the result that she has ever since been mystified by amateur coin tricks, was able to guess the identity of the murderer from the middle of the book.

The cure for boredom is curiosity. There is no cure for curiosity.

The first thing I do in the morning is brush my teeth and sharpen my tongue.

There's a helluva distance between wisecracking and wit. Wit has truth in it; wisecracking is simply calisthenics with words.

The two most beautiful words in the English language are: Check Enclosed.

The best way to keep children at home is to make the home a pleasant atmosphere and let the air out of the tires.

The Monte Carlo casino refused to admit me until I was properly dressed so I went and found my stockings, and then came back and lost my shirt.

Take care of luxuries and the necessities will take care of themselves.

The two most beautiful words in the English language are 'check enclosed.'

The cure for boredom is curiosity. There is no cure for curiosity.

The best way to keep children home is to make the home atmosphere pleasant -- and let the air out of the tires.

That woman speaks eighteen languages, and can't say No in any of them.

That woman speaks eight languages and can't say no in any of them.

They sicken at the calm that know the storm.

This book is not to be tossed lightly aside, but to be hurled with great force.

This wasn't just plain terrible, this was fancy terrible. This was terrible with raisins in it.

Those who have mastered etiquette, who are entirely, impeccably right, would seem to arrive at a point of exquisite dullness.

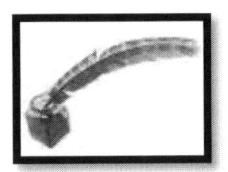

Where's the man could ease a heart, like a satin gown?

Why is it no one ever sent me yet one perfect limousine, do you suppose? Ah no, it's always just my luck to get one perfect rose.

Wit has truth in it; wisecracking is simply calisthenics with words.

Woman to Dorothy: 'I really can't come to your party, I can't bear fools,'
Dorothy to woman: 'That's strange, your mother could.'

Work is the province of cattle.

When your bank account is so overdrawn that it is positively photographic, steps must be taken.

Wit has truth in it; wisecracking is simply calisthenics with words

Women and elephants never forget.

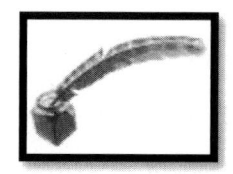

You can't teach an old dogma new tricks.

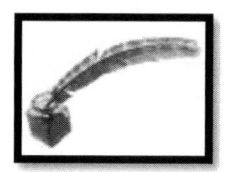

Although she was completely dismissive of her own talents, Dorothy became famous for her short, viciously humorous poems, many about the perceived ludicrousness of her many (largely unsuccessful) romantic affairs and others wistfully considering the appeal of suicide. She survived several suicide attempts, which increased as her dependency on alcohol increased.

'Promises, promises.' **Dorothy when her doctor told her she would be dead in a month if she did not stop drinking**

"As only New Yorkers know, if you can get through the twilight, you'll live through the night."

"It's not the tragedies that kill us, it's the messes."

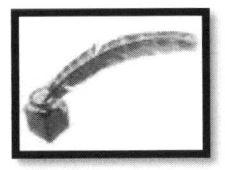

Dorothy Parker Time Line

1893 -- Dorothy was born on August 22. Her merchant family is wealthy and she was left a small but comfortable fortune, something she seldom discussed.

1897 -- Dorothy's mother died.

1913 -- Dorothy's father died.

1914 -- Dorothy published her first poem entitled "Any Porch."

He [Robert Benchley] and I had an office so tiny that an inch smaller and it would have been adultery.

1917 - 1920 -- Dorothy became a staff writer for *Vogue*.

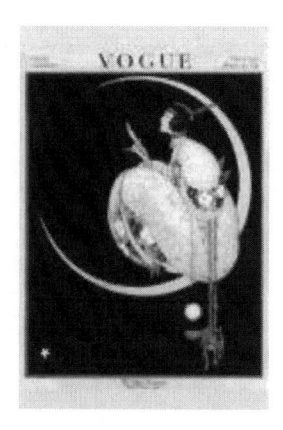

1917 -- Dorothy married Edwin Pond Dorothy II.

1919 -- The Algonquin Round Table met for the first time.

1920 -- Dorothy was fired from Vanity Fair.

1920 - 1923 -- Dorothy contributed essays, poetry, and reviews to Ainslee's, Saturday Evening Post, Ladies' Home Journal, Everybody's, and Life.

1922 -- Dorothy published her first book, Women I'm Not Married To; Men I'm Not Married To.

1925 -- Dorothy worked on her first film script, Business is Business, with George Kaufman.

1926 -- Dorothy published Enough Rope, a collection of poems. It was a best-seller.

1927 - 1931 -- Dorothy contributed fiction, poetry, and reviews to The New Yorker.

1928 -- Dorothy divorced Edwin Dorothy. She also published Sunset Gun, a collection of poetry.

1929 -- Dorothy won the O. Henry Award for her short story "Big Blonde."

1930 -- Dorothy published *Laments for the Living,* a collection of fiction.

1931 -- Dorothy published *Death and Taxes,* a collection of poems.

1933 -- Dorothy published *After Such Pleasures,* a collection of stories.

1934 -- Dorothy married Alan Campbell.

1936 -- Dorothy published *Not so Deep as a Well*, a collection of poetry.

1939 -- Dorothy published *Here Lies*, a collection of stories.

1942 --Dorothy published *Collected Stories*.

1944 -- The Viking Portable Library: Dorothy Parker is published with poems and stories selected by Parker.

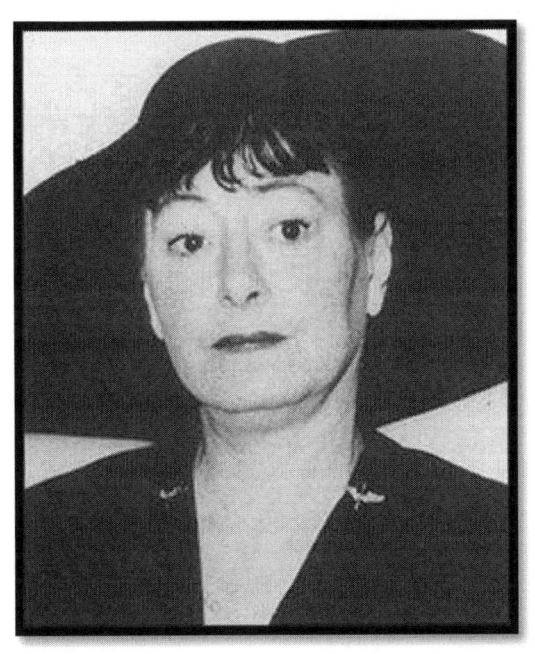

Dorothy wears aviator wings on her dress. At the time, her husband was in the Army Air Corps

1947 -- Dorothy divorced from Alan Campbell.

1950 -- Dorothy remarried Alan Campbell.

1957 - 1963 -- Dorothy served as a book reviewer for **Esquire.**

1958 -- Dorothy published her last short story, "Bolt in the Blue," in *Esquire*.

1959 -- Dorothy inducted into the American Academy of Arts and Letters.

1963 -- Dorothy's husband Alan Campbell committed suicide.

1963 - 1964 -- Dorothy served as the Distinguished Visiting Professor of English at the California State College at L.A.

1964 -- Dorothy published her last magazine piece for *Esquire*.

1967 -- Dorothy died of a heart attack.

A few of Dorothy's Book Reviews

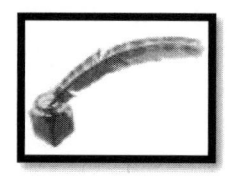

Parker on Kathleen Norris's novel, Beauty and the Beast:

"I'm much better now, in fact, than I was when we started. I wish you could have heard that pretty crash Beauty and the Beast made when, with one sweeping, liquid gesture, I tossed it out of my twelfth-story window."

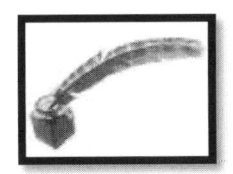

From her review of Caste, a novel by an illustrious gent named Cosmo Hamilton:

"Until today, I walked square-shouldered among my fellows, looking them in the composite eye, and said in unshaken tones: 'Anyway, there are two things I have never done. I never resisted an officer, and I never read anything by Cosmo Hamilton.' Today only the first half of that ringing boast is true. I made, as usual, the wrong selection."

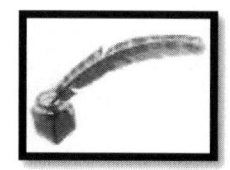

From a theater review in The New Yorker:

"If you want to, you can pick me out of any crowd, these days. I am the little one in the corner who did not think that the 'Barretts of Wimpole Street' was a great play, nor even a good play. It is true that I paid it the tribute of tears, but that says nothing, for I am one who weeps at Victorian costumes."

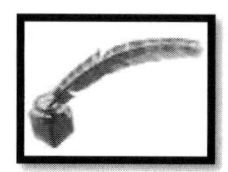

From her review of Nathalie Colby's novel, Black Stream, Parker notes the uncanny similarities to Virginia Woolf's prose:

"In her first few chapters she has so skillfully emphasized the less fortunate mannerisms of her instructress that the strong-minded and generously inclined among her readers give her credit for an admirably sustained and a delicately cruel bit of burlesque."

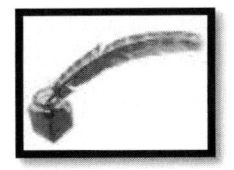

From her review of Will Durant's novel, Transition, she writes:

"Dr. Will Durant, the worst reporter that the Snyder-Gray trial ever had (and that's no faint praise), says of his book, Transition, which has a sub-title 'A Sentimental Story of One Mind and One Era,' that he just dashed it off by way of a holiday. Dr. Will Durant should stick to business."

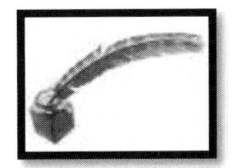

From her review of Sinclair Lewis's novel, Dodsworth:

"I cannot, with the slightest sureness, tell you if it will sweep the country, like 'Main Street,' or bring forth yards of printed praise…My guess would be that it will not. Other guesses I which I have made in the past half-year have been that Al Smith would carry New York state, that St. John Ervine would be a great dramatic critic for an American newspaper, and that I would have more than twenty-six dollars in the bank on March 1st. So you see my my confidence in my judgment is scarcely what it used to be."

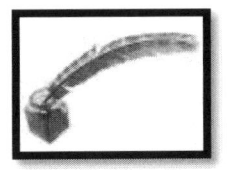

From her essay, "The Wallflowers Lament"

"It has lately been drawn to your correspondent's attention that, at social gatherings, she is not the human magnet she would be. Indeed, it turns out that as a source of entertainment, conviviality, and good fun, she ranks somewhere between a spring of parsley and a single ice skate."

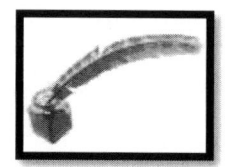

From her review of The Technique of the Love Affair

"You know how you ought to be with men? You should always be aloof, you should never let them know you like them, you must on no account let them feel that they are of any importance to you, you must be wrapped up in your own concerns, you may never let them lose sight of the fact that you are superior, you must be, in short, a regular stuffed chemise. And if you could only see what I've been doing!"

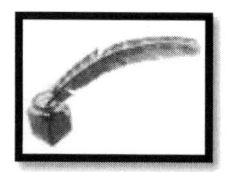

Parker on the novel, Gay Agony

"I tried Gay Agony — eventually these trick titles will get me, and I will be found in a small, quiet place, completely surrounded by iron bars, sitting looking at my hands all day — by H.A. Manhood. Well, if it's the man's name, can I help it?

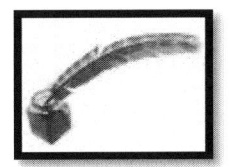

From her review of the Best American Short Stories of 1927

"I read about bored and pampered wives who were right on the verge of eloping with slender-fingered, quizzical-eyed artists, but did not... I read tales proving that Polack servant girls have their feelings, too. I read of young men who collected blue jade, and solved mysterious murders, on the side."

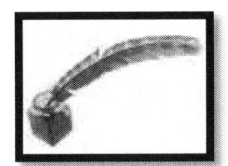

Parker on André Gide

"The Counterfeiters is too tremendous a thing for praises. To say of it, 'Here is a magnificent novel' is rather like gazing into the Grand Canyon and and remarking, 'Well, well, well; quite a slice.' Doubtless you have heard that this book is not pleasant. Neither, for that matter, is the Atlantic Ocean."

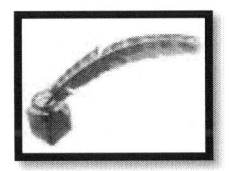

Parker's review of French conversation books

"Annually I drag out the conversation books, and begin that process called brushing up. It always happens about this time, when the wanderlust is as overpowering as the humidity, and I develop my yearly case of the get-away-from-it-alls. And it seems to me only the part of wisdom to dust off the Continental tongues, because you can't tell—maybe any time now one of the steamship lines will listen to reason and accept teeth instead of money, and I will be on my way back to the Old Country."

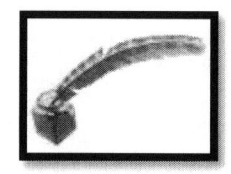

From her review of Robert Hyde's book:

"Crude is the name of Robert Hyde's first novel. It is also a criticism of it."

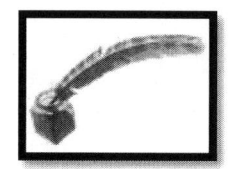

On the use of "hummy" for "honey" in A.A. Milne's The House at Pooh Corner:

"It is that word 'hummy,' my darlings that marks the first place in The House at Pooh Corner at which Tonstant Weader Fwowed up."

You can lead a horticulture, but you can't make her think. **When talking to a ladies gardening group, Dorothy Parker was asked to use the word 'horticulture' in a sentence. Another version of this is that when the difficult actress Joan Crawford was married to the aristocratic Franchot Tone, she became obsessed with self-improvement causing Dorothy to quip "You can take a whore to culture, but you can't make her think."**

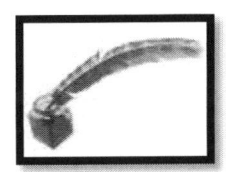

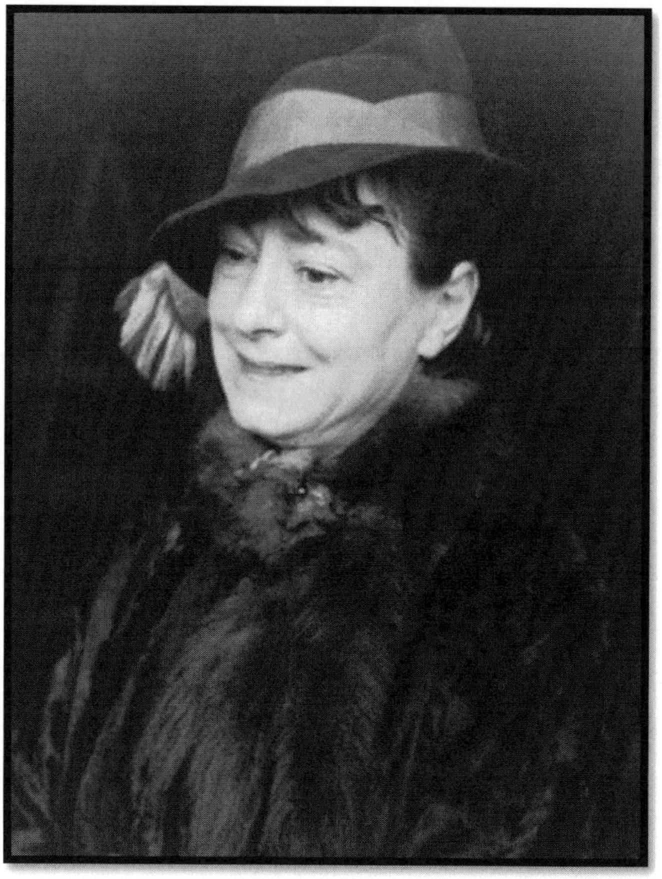

Printed in Great Britain
by Amazon.co.uk, Ltd.,
Marston Gate.